"*Let us be grateful to people who make us happy:*

They are the charming gardeners who make our souls blossom."

Marcel Proust

The Fox Diaries

The Year the Foxes Came to our Garden

Valarie Budayr

Audrey Press
Maryville, Tennessee

Publisher's Cataloging-in-Publication Data
Budayr, Valarie.
The fox diaries : the year the foxes came to our garden / Valarie Budayr. – p. cm.
Includes bibliographical references.
ISBN 978-1-936426-18-8
[1. Foxes. 2. Foxes–Behavior. 3. Foxes–Habits and behavior. 4. Foxes –North America.] I. Title.

QL737.C22   B83 2011 [599.775]–dc22   2011900978

Valarie Budayr
P.O. Box 6113
Maryville, TN 37802
Valarie@audreypress.com
www.valariebudayr.com
www.jumpintoabook.com
www.learnsweden.com

Printed in the United States by BookMasters, Inc.
30 Amberwood Parkway
Ashland, Ohio 44805
March 2011, Job #M8267

E 599.775 Bud

*I lovingly dedicate this book to my children
and to my husband who, alongside me,
experienced the awe and wonder of living with foxes.*

With much gratitude I would like to recognize the incredible people who have inspired me to live the dream of writing and envisioning books.

First and foremost, many thanks go to my parents, who instilled in all their children, "You can do anything that your mind can think up." Here is proof of such an endeavor.

My husband, Mahdi, who has believed in this project from the first moment we spotted the foxes. Thanks for always believing in my next creative project. It helps so very much to have a cheering section.

To my children, Zuzu, Mimi, and Opus, great creators of magical moments, I love every minute we spend together. Here's to us and everything and anything we can think up.

Many thanks and love goes to our large extended families. I would love to write all of your names but the book isn't long enough. We love you all the same.

Best friends are forever, and mine are Susie and Ruthie. Thanks for a million and one laughs throughout the years.

To the Rosemen, Huckleberry, E, and Seppie. Family first and foremost, thanks for all of the memories, vacations, business ideas, music, creative endeavors, feasts and above all else, through thick and through thin, just plain living.

To Lawrence of Maryville and the ever lovely Gillian, our family celebrations wouldn't be the same without you. Cheers!

To Chaoxing and Kathy, I don't think I know two more compassionate people than you. I cherish your friendship so very much. Thank you for creating holidays, Chinese feasts, and lovely tea time on Sundays and for sharing your boys Michael and Nathan with us.

Many thanks go to Per Svangren for being an incredible business partner and friend. I cherish the many traditions our families share and look forward to our future endeavors, whatever those may be.

I cannot ask for better friends than the whole Svangren family. Lotta, I love crafting, gardening, touring, and drinking coffee with you. Thank you for always welcoming us to your home and making every moment memorable. Rebi Tucker, Signatore, Johannes and Anna, oh and of course Diesel and Ninja, thanks for being you. I love the time we spend together.

To Heather and Bernadette, from the bottom of my heart, thank you for creating such a wonderful magazine and for a very creative platform to share our ideas.

To my assistants Caley Walsh and Terry Green, thank you for helping me bring into being all of the ideas in my head. Simply put, I could not do it without you.

Jenny, I'm so glad that we are still friends after 25 years and that you have moved up the street from me. I treasure every minute I spend with you Georgie, Lilla Mimi, and Paul. It's an honor to play "Auntie" to your family. Here's to many happy years ahead.

To my editor Sibohan Gallagher, thank you for putting the polish on this heartfelt project. Thank you for the great care you have shown.

To one very talented designer Roscoe Welply. Thank you for shepherding into being the ideas and vision of this book.

To my neighbors who showed great enthusiasm and love for our little fox family.

To all of the readers of my blog "A Place Like This", it was so special that we could share this together. I love that we have such a creative community via the blogosphere. I am grateful for each one of you who stops by the blog and am truly inspired by your presence there.

Table of Contents~

The Sleeping Fox:
Winter

Every morning I would walk down to the kitchen to spy a fox through the window lying underneath our tree. Each day, she would notice me too, and sit on the hill looking into our kitchen, just watching. After a time, she would walk away.

After several weeks of this, one day she disappeared. Every morning when I came downstairs, I would look for her. But she wasn't there.

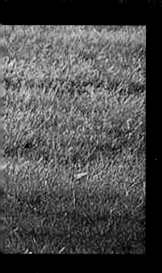

And Now There Are Five

One February morning, as I sat at my desk, I spotted her. My beautiful fox was sitting out on our front lawn.

To my surprise, four little kits, her baby foxes, came running up to her.

Evening~

The fox and her kits returned. My children and I sat quietly on the front porch, eyes glued, careful not to disturb them.

It was a magical moment for us, sitting there on our porch as the sun slowly set, watching the little fox family frolic in the front yard.

One Week~

It's been exactly one week now since I sat that day at my desk writing, and spied the beautiful momma fox and her four babies.

We see the little fox family twice each day now, every day, in the early morning as the sun rises, and again at dusk as the sun sinks below the horizon.

We've come to know them—their distinctive fur markings, their mannerisms, their personalities.

Now it's time for you to meet our special garden guests.

Momma Rennie~

Momma Rennie, as we have come to call her, is a symbol of calmness and grace. She gives her babies a lot of freedom to explore, and spends countless hours every day teaching them how to survive.

While the small kits sleep in their cozy den, Momma Rennie will often pass by me working in the garden as she gathers food to feed her growing family.

Hulda~

Hulda, one of the kits, is the quiet one of the family. She is very shy and fearful of many things, including some of her very own family members. She spends most of her time in the den, coming out for only short periods of time in the afternoon.

Osa & Effie~

Osa and Effie are inseparable. Always together, always playing, and always tumbling over each other. They are completely immersed in their own world. Every now and then they will check to see where Momma Rennie is, but for the most part they are velcroed to each other.

They make us laugh with their funny antics. They are also the two that try and sneak out of the den, while everyone else is sleeping.

Ring-Ding~

And then there is Ring-Ding.

We call him that because he seems to be constantly hungry. He runs circles around his mother, always begging for food. Momma Rennie is always calm and ignores him. She just walks away, even when he bites her tail and hangs on for the ride.

The Big Dig

In our front yard, there are big holes on either side of the driveway. All these have been dug, of course, by our garden guests. Every day, I sit on our lawn and watch as Momma Rennie imparts new skills to her young skulk. A skulk is a family group of foxes. They are learning how to dig.

A good digging spot~

With her skilled eye, Momma Rennie looks for the perfect place to dig—a place where the earth isn't compacted too tightly, the perfect place for little paws to practice.

When she selects the ideal spot, she starts to dig. Her four little kits watch her intently from their safe spot on the sidelines.

Working Together~

With nothing more than a look and a single yip to ensure their complete attention, she signals to her young,

"Who'll be first?

Who wants to give it a try?"

Osa and Effie are first to answer the call.

Ring-Ding and Hulda sit back on the sidelines, content to simply watch for the moment.

Momma Rennie keeps checking the hole to see if it's deep enough and is being dug in the right direction.

After each inspection, she makes little adjustments with her young ones looking on. The kit who was digging then mimics her exact movements and delights in her approval.

Our Turn~

Hulda and Ring-Ding come closer to take another look before heading to the opposite side of the yard to start a hole of their very own.

Osa and Effie are excited to learn this new skill. They keep digging, their little paws churning up the dirt.

This beautifully dug hole is the result.
The kits are excited and Momma Rennie is satisfied.

Coming Out

Foxes dig for several important reasons. They must learn how to hide their food. Foxes hunt even when they aren't hungry and then they bury their food to eat later. All night long they hunt, only going to bed just after the sun begins to rise.

Foxes also dig to build themselves a home. They dig their dens into the earth and later enlarge them when they need to. Each momma fox digs as many as three or four different dens while she is pregnant. This way she can move her family from den to den to ensure they stay safe and protected from predators which

Afternoon ritual~

Every afternoon at two o'clock sharp, I get a glimpse of two little ears peeking out from the opening of the den. They belong to Hulda. She is the most timid of the group and she likes her alone time. While her siblings are slumbering, Hulda creeps out and takes an hour or so for herself.

Always making sure she stays very near the den, in case she needs to make a quick escape, Hulda contentedly plays, lounges, and investigates her world all by herself.

Foxes sleep during the day. So why is this little fox awake and looking at me?
Well, if you know anything about babies, they do not sleep when the rest of the world
does!

It is always a big event when the kits
enter the outside world after a day of
sleep. Normal wakeup time is 6:30
in the evening.

Hulda and Ring-Ding are always the
first kits to emerge from the den.

They need to move quickly out of the way because here come Osa and Effie!

Where's Mom?~

So, after their grand entrance and daily greetings, it's time to look for Momma Rennie.

"Where's Mom?"

There she is!
She's over there, in the flowers.

With great affection and longing, Ring-Ding
runs to his mother.
No doubt he's hungry again!
"Hi, Mom! I missed you!" says Ring-Ding.

Teamwork

As another day for us is ending, our foxes have made their daily entry into the outside world.

Three of the little kits have been hunting on their own for a few days now. Momma Rennie, knowing that the survival of her kits depends on their being able to hunt for themselves, teaches them to hunt in pairs. Hunting in pairs is both safer and more successful.

Learning to hunt~

First, Momma Rennie calls Ring-Ding over to her.

Then she calls Hulda to join Ring-Ding. Since Osa and Effie have always been a team, they are natural hunting buddies.

To make sure they understand that they are now a group, she throws a dead squirrel into the hole that the kits have dug the day before.

These babies are very competitive and fight to prevent each other from entering the hole to get the squirrel.

After many tumbles, yips, and tugs, Hulda is victorious!.

Hulda will be the first to hunt, as Ring-Ding calls to her from the sidelines. Foxes hunt by talking to their partners in high-pitched screams.

Hulda's hunt~

Hulda stands with Momma Rennie, scoping out a variety of prey. Soon they target a squirrel.

Osa and Effie watch attentively to see if Hulda, the timid one, is really going to do it.

Momma Rennie and Ring-Ding stand ready at the sidelines to give Hulda support if she needs it.

Off Hulda creeps, quietly sneaking up on her unsuspecting prey.

Not sure if she is doing it right, she glances over at Effie and Osa, who are yipping excitedly, watching.

"Is this the right squirrel over here, Mom?" asks an anxious Hulda.

The big scare~

Just as she gets encouragement from Momma Rennie, the neighbor's dog spots Hulda from behind the fence and starts barking frantically. This, of course, scares the wits out of our poor Hulda and sends her running in the opposite direction, the squirrel now forgotten.

"Did you hear that, Mom?" pants Hulda.

Momma Rennie patiently comforts her little kit.

All the while, the observing brother and sister, Osa and Effie, chatter wildly.

"That didn't go so well, did it?" says Effie.

"Well, I'll have you know, if that had been me...,
I would have razzle-dazzled them!" boasts Osa.

Playing Tag

Although the games the kits engage in look like random play, it's actually play with a purpose.

Can you spot the wily fox in this photo?

Hiding~

Foxes use a variety of skills to catch their prey.
The first is being in plain sight without being seen.

Endurance~

The next great skill is endurance.
Foxes aren't swift chasers like wolves or cougars, but if you've ever seen one chasing a bunny, you know that endurance is a great skill in a fox's hunting tool kit.

"Well, not for very long.
You had all better run really fast!"

After Hulda tags Osa, there is a lot of yipping and calling out.

And then there is a lot of running, with Osa chasing quickly behind.

After many long minutes of running around the yard and tagging each other, they are finally looking rather tired.

One sad little face seems to be saying, "But I didn't get to be IT."

Effie wasn't IT during the entire game of tag. She outran all her siblings and was never once caught.

Now there's a swift, sly fox if ever there was one!

Hide 'n Seek

"Now where could they be?"

"I found you, Effie. Now help me find the others."

Looking around, Osa heads off towards the end of the stick pile. What he doesn't realize is that the rules have suddenly changed and now he is the one they're searching for.

"Whew! That was close. I guess I outfoxed them!"

"Hey! Where is everyone?"

"Hello-o-o-o?"

"I guess I'll just have to sniff them out."

"Aha! There they are!"

"I'd like to propose a game change," announces Osa.

In and Out

"Let's play in and out of the sticks...

You can only go in and out. You can't climb over them."

Even though the young foxes go out and practice their hunting skills by playing these fun games, Mom and Dad still bring them their food.

Everything Momma Rennie has taught them is designed to make them more and more independent every day. Someday soon, they will leave Momma Rennie and search for their own territory to hunt in. Perhaps they, too, will have families of their own, and teach their little kits the skills that Momma Rennie has taught them. But for now they are still living happily in our garden!

A Few Things to Know About Foxes

A few things to know about foxes~

My family took the occasion of having a fox family living in the front yard to do a little research about these wonderful animals. Throughout time, the fox has developed the reputation of being a menace, uninvited and unwelcome. Increased development has destroyed much of their natural habitat, as it has with many wildlife, shrinking their territory and forcing them to venture beyond, into residential areas. Watching this little family grow revealed to us that living with foxes is an awe-inspiring event which has forged for us a connection with nature like nothing we've ever experienced.

Where is the red fox found?

The red fox is the largest of the fox breeds and can be found throughout the world, as far north as the Arctic Circle and on down through Europe, North and Central America, Northern Africa and parts of Asia.

What makes a fox unique?

The fox has a very long body and very short legs. Its tail, called a brush, is longer than half of its body size. It acts like a cat's tail to give it balance while running and jumping. A fox will also curl its tail around its face to keep it warm while sleeping. A fox's feet are very special. They have five digits (rather like our fingers) on their front paws and four digits on their back paws. This allows them to move very quickly and silently, as well as to jump very high. A fox can jump up to six feet high, which will easily get him over most fences.

Fox tracks

Do foxes live alone or do they live in groups?

The answer to this is yes and no. Between the months of August/September and January, foxes live a solitary life. Come December, they select a mate and start a family. From February until August, they live and hunt in their family groups, which are called skulks. The female fox is called a vixen and the male fox is called a dog. Baby foxes are called cubs or kits.

Where do foxes live?

Foxes live in dens. These are burrows under the ground. They often dig their dens into hills, ravines, ditches, gutters and beneath tree roots. Red fox dens are divided into separate little rooms, called burrows. The fox is an incredible digger and can move soil quickly by moving first the dirt with the forepaws and then kicking that same dirt with the hind legs. The main passageway of the den is about fifty-five feet long and ranges between four and eight feet in height.

Before a vixen gives birth to her young, it isn't uncommon for her to dig four or five different dens so she can relocate her family swiftly and easily. Foxes may also share their dens with large woodchucks and or badgers.

After the kits have grown and are out of the den, most foxes prefer to abandon the den in favor of living outside, in the forest or in heavy brush.

How large is a fox family or skulk?

A fox skulk consists of a vixen, a dog and their kits. A group of kits born together is called a litter. It is also common to have the previous year's kits, who are now grown, hunting in the same area, often with their original family. They will not have their own kits until they establish a new hunting territory.

How large is a litter?

The average litter size is four to six kits. Kits are born unable to see or hear, and they have no teeth; they have dark brown, fluffy fur. The vixen remains with the kits in the den for two to three weeks to keep them warm and feed them. The dog, or father, brings food for the vixen to eat so that she doesn't have to leave her babies.
If, for some reason, the mother fox should die during the nurturing period, the dog will take over and raise the kits.

How do kits change as they grow?

The kits' eyes open, and their teeth appear after two weeks. At about three weeks, the color of their coats starts to change, and black eye streaks begin to appear. At four weeks, red and white patches appear on their faces and their ears point straight up. Kits leave the den at this point, and the vixen and dog start feeding the litter solid food. By the time they are eight weeks old, they are eating completely solid food and no longer require their mother's milk.
As they continue to grow, their fur becomes very red. They learn to hunt and bury their food, as well as dig their dens. By the time a fox is five to six months old, they resemble an adult fox. They stay with their skulk until they are seven or eight months of age. At that stage, many will leave their families and find new hunting territories of their own.

A fox will be ready to start their own family by the time they are ten months old.

What do foxes eat?

Red foxes are omnivores, just like humans, eating both plants and meat. They prey upon small animals, including voles, mice, squirrels, rabbits, deer mice, birds, reptiles and insects. They target animals that typically weigh less than seven pounds.

Foxes do not eat cats.

If you have ever tried to give a cat a pill, you will know why a fox gives a cat a wide berth. A cat has teeth and claws, and is as limber as a fox. Simply, it is just too much work. Foxes and the family dog will not get along at all.

Foxes also like to eat a variety of plants and in some areas will feed exclusively on fruit during the months of August and September. Blackberries, raspberries, cherries, mulberries, apples, plums, grapes, and nuts make up a favorite meal for a fox. A fox needs to eat one pound of food a day to remain healthy. If foxes live proximal to humans, they will also eat garbage. It is important to remember to close garbage cans tightly and never to feed any wild animal. The moment a wild animal eats human food, they become a nuisance, putting both animal and humans at risk.

What makes foxes good hunters?

Their hearing is exceptional. They can actually hear a bird fly, and land on a bush from a quarter-mile away. They can hear a hen moving on its roost from 500 feet away. Just because a mouse lives underground, doesn't mean a fox can't hear it. The fox can hear it move up to 330 feet underneath the earth. It then uses its digging skills to quickly capture its prey.

In our yard, we often witnessed the foxes targeting and hunting squirrels. They would single out their prey and sneak up on it. As the squirrel became aware of the fox's presence, the fox would begin to dance, leaping high into the air with funny twists caused by twitching its tail. Each little turn would position the fox a little bit closer to the squirrel which would watch the fox, entranced. Eventually, the fox would get close enough to the unsuspecting squirrel to catch it with one quick snap.

How do foxes hunt?

Our fox family hunted in a group. They preferred to hunt in the late evening, returning only at sunrise. Oftentimes they would bring back their prey and bury it in the front yard to eat later. There were often mounds of dirt scattered all over the front and side yards. The squirrel and rabbit population dwindled quickly, and likely accounts for why they relocated to another den in early summer. It takes a lot of food to feed a family of six foxes.

Do foxes talk?

Yes, they do. Along with body language, foxes communicate through vocal sounds. They have a five-octave vocal range which produces twelve different sounds for the adults and eight different sounds in the kits.

Greetings

When two foxes approach one another, they make a barking sound which resembles the hoot of an owl. We observed three quick barks, hoo, hoo, hoo. We saw the kits do this as well with each other. Once their greetings were given, they made a warbling sound in their throats as a sign of recognition. Rennie, our momma fox, would acknowledge her kits with a big huff every time they approached.

SOS Call

When a fox encounters an animal that might want to eat them, like a dog or a coyote, the fox lets off a shrill loud scream. If the encounter becomes aggressive, they emit a loud rattle in their throat, called gekkering. If the attacking animal should get too close, the fox will bark, just like a dog.

Love Song

A vixen howls a love song to find a mate. It's a long held cry of awwwwwwwww. If she receives more than one reply, she will emit that deep, throaty rattle, called gekkering, to dismiss those dogs she does not want.

Glossary~

brush: the bushy tail of a fox

dog: a male fox

fox face: the pointy muzzle of a fox

gekkering: a throaty rattle when under attack or during mating season

kit: a baby fox (also referred to as a cub or pup)

litter: babies born to the same parents at one time

skulk: a family or hunting group of foxes

vixen: a female fox

Resources~

◆ **Red Fox National Geographic**
http://animals.nationalgeographic.com/animals/mammals/red-fox.html

◆ **Natural History of the Red Fox by Wildlife Online**
http://www.wilklifeonline.me.uk/red_fox.html

◆ **Wikipedia: Red Fox**
http://en.wikipedia.org/wiki/red_fox

Favorite Fox Movies~

◆ The Fox and The Hound (1981)

◆ The Fox and the Child (2007)

◆ Fantastic Mr. Fox (2009)

About the Author~

Valarie Budayr is a Renaissance woman, embracing and encompassing many talents. For over 15 years she taught piano, and was a two-time NEA "Meet the Composer" grant winner. For the last four years, she has been co-owner and marketing director for LearnSweden, an online language company. Along with her love of music, she enjoys working with fiber, especially wool, travelling with her family, crafting, bio-diverse gardening, and above and foremost, possesses a great love of books. Valarie has been a frequent contributor to the online magazine, Rhythm of the Home. You can find Valarie's daily writings, creative and crafty living, photography, and book adventures on her popular blogs:

A Place like This   www.valariebudayr.com
LearnSweden   www.learnsweden.com
Jump into a Book   www.jumpintoabook.com